GRIT

\ grit \

firmness of mind or spirit;
unyielding courage in the
face of hardship or danger[1]

Published by Bushel & Peck Books, a family-run publishing house in Fresno, California, that
believes in uplifting children with the highest standards of art, music, literature, and ideas.
Find beautiful books for gifted young minds at www.bushelandpeckbooks.com.

Type set in Century Schoolbook, Active, Special Elite, and Papercute.

Illustrations are mixed-media digital collages with elements sourced from
public domain galleries or licensed from Shutterstock.com.

Bushel & Peck Books is dedicated to fighting illiteracy all over the world.
For every book we sell, we donate one to a child in need—book for book.
To nominate a school or organization to receive free books,
please visit www.bushelandpeckbooks.com.

LCCN: 2021943568
ISBN: 9781638191025

First Edition

Printed in the United States

10 9 8 7 6 5 4 3 2 1

GRIT

INSPIRING STORIES FOR WHEN THE GOING GETS TOUGH

S.E. ABRAMSON

BUSHEL
& PECK
BOOKS

Publisher's Note

Dear reader,

Challenges come to us all in many shapes and sizes. At first, they might make us want to run away, or dive under the covers, or hide under the bed and never come out until the difficulty passes. If you feel that way, you're not alone!

But as you read these pages, perhaps a new idea will occur to you. Could it be, just maybe, that some of the hard things in life are actually something to . . . celebrate?

In this book, you'll discover eighteen heroes who faced challenges of their own. You'll hear stories about physical limitations, racial prejudice, mental health, family challenges, gender ceilings, nearly failed businesses, and more. These are hard things, no doubt about it, and some aren't easy to talk about. Some seem so unfair that it's hard to see how *anything* good might come from them. But take heart, because in these same stories, you'll hear remarkable tales of courage, determination, grit, and what can happen if one pushes through until the storm passes. Most exciting of all, you'll discover the life-changing truth that challenges:

- can be stepping-stones to new successes.
- can help us develop skills and characteristics gained no other way.
- can instill compassion and empathy for those around us.
- can open doors to new opportunities.
- can be the common experience that brings us all together.

So take courage, dear reader. You are not alone. With grit and determination, you can get through life's tough moments and even turn them to your good. Read on, and let's find that grit together! We're rooting for you.

Sincerely,

Bushel & Peck Books

Contents

EIGHTEEN HEROES WHO HAD GRIT

LUDWIG VAN BEETHOVEN

DECEMBER 16, 1770-MARCH 26, 1827

The musician who never gave up.

Ludwig van Beethoven began to learn music when he was just five years old in his hometown of Bonn, Germany. His father, Johann, was a harsh teacher, often reducing his son to tears. However, Ludwig was talented and he worked very hard. He later learned from composer and conductor Christian Gottlob Neefe and eventually found respite from his turbulent home under the friendship and employment of Helene von Breuning, an

If he couldn't compose with his ears, he would compose with his imagination.

upper-class citizen of Bonn, who hired him to teach piano to her children. In time, more opportunities for Ludwig's talent came, and he quickly became one of Europe's most celebrated composers.

But suddenly, just when he was at the height of his career, Ludwig began to have problems with his hearing. Over a slow period of time, he became increasingly deaf and developed mild tinnitus (ringing in the ears).

No hearing? It might have spelled doom for a musician like Ludwig, but he was no stranger to hardship. Though tremendously discouraged, Ludwig determined to push through. After all, he could still hear melodies in his mind. If he couldn't compose with his ears, he would compose with his imagination. As he had remarked earlier in life, "What I have in my heart must out; that is why I write."[3]

Ludwig van Beethoven went on to become one of the most well-known and beloved classical music composers of all time. In fact, some of his greatest works were composed *after* his hearing began to fade. He saw great success and popularity during his lifetime, and his legacy continued even after his death in 1827. His works remain among the most frequently performed pieces of classical music and include famous songs such as *Symphony No. 5* ("Beethoven's Fifth"), *Moonlight Sonata*, and *Für Elise*.

Imagine that you're a famous composer and have started losing your hearing. How might you feel? Would you want to give up?

How do you think Ludwig found his determination to continue on? What might you tell yourself when *you* need help continuing on?

JESSE OWENS

The athlete who competed for more than gold.

From a young age, Jesse was a gifted athlete. His junior high school track coach allowed him to practice before school so that he could work in the afternoons. While he was still in high school, he matched the world record for the 100-meter dash, running it in only 9.4 seconds. On May 25, 1935, when Jesse was in college, he broke not just one but *four* world records: the 100-yard dash, the long jump, the 220-yard sprint, and the 220-yard low hurdles.

Though Jesse was talented and enjoyed success on the Ohio State University track team, he still faced discrimination for being Black. Most athletes at Ohio State were given on-campus housing, but Jesse had to find off-campus housing with other Black students. When the track team traveled to competitions away from school, he had to eat at different restaurants and stay in different hotels from the rest of his teammates. And despite being arguably more gifted than his teammates, Jesse did not have an athletic scholarship at Ohio State and had to work part-time jobs in order to keep himself in school.

With his athletic prowess, Jesse qualified for the 1936 Olympics in Berlin, Germany. However, he almost didn't go. He and other Black Olympian athletes felt that Black Americans should not participate in an event in Germany, which at the time was under Nazi control and heavily racist. However, after some pressure from the United States Olympic committee, Jesse and the other Olympians decided to go after all. Despite Nazi propaganda against Jesse and Black athletes, Jesse proved very popular with the German people. During the Olympic games, Jesse would win four gold medals for America in track and field. This record wasn't beaten or even matched until 1984!

After the Olympics, Jesse wanted to take up some paid endorsement opportunities. However, prejudiced

US athletic officials decided to withdraw Jesse's "amateur" status, which effectively ended his career as an athlete. Though he came home from the Olympics with four gold medals, he struggled to find work for some time. Jesse took on menial jobs like gas station attendant and janitor. He occasionally raced people and even horses for cash. After years of struggling to make ends meet, Jesse was finally appointed by the United States as a goodwill ambassador, and he spoke to countries and companies to inspire people around the world.

For his whole life, Jesse had to work harder than white athletes to receive even the same amount of recognition. Discrimination made it impossible for him to make a full career out of his talents simply because other people thought that the color of his skin made him an inferior person. But today, Jesse is remembered as the talented athlete he was and for what he showed the world at a time that Black athletes were still fighting for respect.

How do you think Jesse felt when he was treated so differently from his teammates? Why didn't this stop him from pursuing his best as an athlete?

CORRIE TEN BOOM

APRIL 15, 1892–APRIL 15, 1983

The prisoner who stayed positive.

I t was 1942, World War II was raging, and German Nazi forces were surging throughout Europe. They were ordered to round up Jews and send them to concentration camps.

It was then that a Jewish woman came knocking at the door of Corrie ten Boom's family home in the Netherlands seeking refuge. She had heard how the Ten Booms had helped their Jewish neighbors before, and now she was in desperate need herself.

Corrie and her family knew they had to help.

The woman would become one of nearly 800 Jews that Corrie and her family helped rescue from the Germans. The Dutch Resistance—a group of locals who fought against the German occupation—heard what the Ten Booms were doing and sent an architect to help them build a secret room in their house. The room would be able to hide Jewish refugees or members of the resistance if the Gestapo—the German secret police—came to search the house. The room became known as "The Hiding Place" to Corrie, her sister Betsie, and everyone else who used the room over the next two years.

But what started as a dangerous situation soon became a perilous one. On February 28, 1944, Corrie and Betsie were arrested by the Gestapo and immediately taken to prison. They were eventually sent to Ravensbrück, a labor concentration camp in Germany. The work was hard, the guards were cruel, and the barracks where they slept were filthy and infested with fleas.

But Corrie and Betsie never gave up. They smuggled a Bible into the camp with them and did their best to lift the spirits of the other women in their barracks by holding worship services after each day's hard work. Sadly, Betsie didn't make it to the end of the war. She died on December 16, 1944. Then, just twelve days after Betsie died, Corrie was released from Ravensbrück. She would later learn that she was released by accident; there was a clerical error in the paperwork around her barracks.

Corrie spent her life working to help those around her. In 1946, after the war had ended, she even returned to Germany to forgive two of the guards who had been at Ravensbrück. Corrie became a public speaker, traveling to over sixty countries to inspire others with stories of hope, optimism, and love in the face of hardship.

How do you think Corrie and Betsie stayed positive during such a difficult time?

What might you be able to do when you feel discouraged?

ELIZABETH BLACKWELL

FEBRUARY 3, 1821–MAY 31, 1910

The medical graduate who found a way.

Elizabeth Blackwell's parents believed that all of their children should be able to follow their dreams and develop their talents. It was a marvelous sentiment, but at first, life didn't work out that way. When Elizabeth was only seventeen years old, her father died, leaving the family in need of a steady income. Unfortunately, the burden fell to Elizabeth and her siblings.

At first, Elizabeth helped her sisters teach school. But after a brief time, Elizabeth decided

If the school wouldn't take her, she'd find one somewhere else that would.

that she wanted to save up money to attend medical school. It was a daunting dream, for once again, things weren't in Elizabeth's favor. At this time in America, all doctors were men. When Elizabeth tried to apply to medical schools in the city of Philadelphia, she was told that she should either go to Paris, or that she should disguise herself as a man. She was determined to do neither. If the schools in Philadelphia wouldn't take her, she'd find one somewhere else in America that would.

Eventually, Elizabeth was accepted into Geneva Medical College in the town of Geneva, New York. But even then, many were skeptical of this young female student. She later wrote, "When I entered college in 1847, the ladies of the town pronounced the undertaking crazy, or worse, and declared that they would die rather than employ a woman a physician."[7] Undaunted, she studied there for two years.

In the summer between those two years, she moved back to Philadelphia and found work in Blockley Almshouse. Blockley Almshouse was both a hospital and a homeless shelter. Elizabeth treated many people suffering from a disease called typhus. It was a lifechanging experience, and Elizabeth wrote her thesis paper on how people with less money were more likely to get sick because they couldn't afford to take care of themselves. She would go on to write many more papers about similar social and medical issues.

After tremendous hard work, on January 23, 1849, at the age of twenty-eight, Elizabeth finally became the first woman to earn a medical degree in the United States of America. Her perseverance blazed a trail for many more women after her.

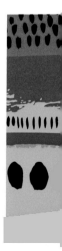

Have you ever had a dream that seemed impossible? What does Elizabeth's experience teach you about finding a way through?

It took years before Elizabeth was able to earn her medical degree. Some things in life require a tremendous amount of patience before they come. What should a person try to remember to help them be patient?

ELLEN DEGENERES

JANUARY 26, 1958–PRESENT

The comedian who turned lemons into lemonade.

You might know Ellen DeGeneres as the funny comedian behind Dory in *Finding Nemo,* but Ellen's childhood was anything but comical. Her parents divorced when she was a teenager, and Ellen's new stepfather mistreated her. Her mother was often very sad. It wasn't an easy time for Ellen, but remarkably, it was her hardships that led her way to humor.

To cheer her mother up when she was depressed, Ellen would tell funny stories. "My mother was going through some really hard times and I could see when she was really getting down, and I would start to make fun of her dancing. Then she'd start to laugh and I'd make fun of her laughing. And she'd laugh so hard she'd start to cry, and then I'd make fun of that. So I would totally bring her from where I'd seen her start going into depression to all the way out of it."[9]

It turned out her mother wasn't the only one who thought Ellen was funny. Ellen eventually began a career as a stand-up comedian, and even then, her difficult past proved a blessing in disguise. She based many of her jokes and stories on tough things that had happened to her, and as a result, people thought that Ellen was funny and relatable. She

Her difficult past proved a blessing in disguise.

was soon promoted to become the emcee of Clyde's Comedy Club in New Orleans, Louisiana.

In 2003, Ellen began her well-known daytime talk show, *The Ellen DeGeneres Show*. It was successful from the beginning, drawing celebrity guests and viral media stars. Ellen became known for singing and dancing at the beginning of the show and during commercial breaks to entertain the studio audience, just like she had for her mother so many years before. She often gave away sponsored prizes and trips to people in the audience and announced donations to charitable causes.

Today, Ellen is one of the most well-known and beloved celebrities in the world. She is open about the difficulties she's faced, and with characteristic wit and humor, she uses her experiences to uplift others around her.

How did some of Ellen's challenges help her develop some of her strengths?

Think of a challenge you might experience in life. Can you see ways it might help you develop strengths in other areas?

WALT DISNEY

DECEMBER 5, 1901–DECEMBER 15, 1966

The visionary who stuck with it.

At only ten years old, Walt Disney rose each morning at 4:30 with his brother Roy so that they could deliver the morning editions of *The Kansas City Times* and *The Kansas City Star*. Then, after school, they would deliver the evening paper in the same way. Sometimes Walt was so tired that he fell asleep in school and his grades suffered, but he kept at his paper route for six years. His ability to stick with something hard would be the key to his success later in life.

From a very young age, Walt was interested in art and drawing. He practiced drawing by copying the cartoons from the front page of another newspaper called *Appeal to Reason*. In high school, Walt took Saturday classes at the Kansas City Art Institute. He also took a correspondence course in cartooning. In 1918, when Walt was just seventeen years old, he joined the Red Cross as an ambulance driver during World War I. Ever the artist, Walt drew cartoons on the side of his ambulance and submitted some of his work for publication in the army newspaper, *Stars and Stripes*.

After World War I ended, Walt worked as an apprentice artist at a commercial art studio. But Walt was eager to start his own business and create his own cartoons. In the following years, he managed to produce small, animated cartoons, which he sold here and there to various advertising companies. Finally, in 1923, Walt's dream was realized when he and his brother Roy formed the Disney Brothers Studio (which would later become The Walt Disney Company).

Running a business proved difficult. Over the years, financial pressures threatened to capsize the company. But the brothers pressed on, and Walt's creativity mixed with Roy's business sense proved a winning combination.

Walt continued to create short animations with sound until 1934, when he began production on his first full-length, animated movie: *Snow White and the Seven Dwarves*. The film was a gamble. Would people even want to see a full-length animated film? On top of that, production costs were an expensive 1.5 million dollars—almost three times over budget.

The risk and perseverance paid off. When *Snow White* was released in 1937, it earned 6.5 million dollars, making it the most successful sound film ever made at the time.

Walt would apply his drive and determination throughout the rest of his life, transforming film, entertainment, and amusement parks with hard work and vision. And perhaps, for all his blockbuster tales on screen, that grit was his greatest story of all.

Delivering papers at such a young age must have been difficult for Walt. How do you think his early experiences with hard work helped him later in life?

Is there something in your life that requires extra work to get right? What can you learn from Walt's life about the importance of working hard?

KATHERINE JOHNSON

AUGUST 26, 1918–FEBRUARY 24, 2020

The math whiz who broke barriers.

Katherine Johnson always had a gift for mathematics. As a student, she worked hard and was able to graduate from high school at just fourteen years of age. She then enrolled at West Virginia State, taking every math class that the college had to offer. At the age of eighteen, Katherine graduated summa cum laude, or "with highest honors," with degrees in mathematics and French.

Katherine worked as a teacher for some time before raising her family. She decided that she wanted to be a research mathematician and began to look for work. A family member told her that the National Advisory Committee for Aeronautics (NACA, later NASA) was hiring Black mathematicians as well as white ones. Katherine began working for NACA in 1953.

At first, Katherine was a "computer." This meant that she solved—*computed*—math problems. Katherine and other computers were assigned to read black box data from airplanes and perform precise calculations based on that data. One day, however, the all-male flight research team borrowed Katherine and a colleague for what was meant to be a temporary assignment. However, Katherine's knowledge of analytic geometry served her well, and the members of the flight research team were so impressed that they made her assignment permanent.

At the time of Katherine's employment for NACA, there were still segregation laws that prevented Black employees from using the same bathrooms or eating in the same places as white employees. Eventually, NASA desegregated many of the work areas, but there were still racial and gender divides within Katherine's workplace. She endured racism and sexism with patience and dignity.

From 1958 until she retired, Katherine worked

as an aerospace technologist for NASA. She even calculated the flight trajectory for the May 5, 1961 space flight of Alan Shepard, the first American in space. One of Katherine's jobs was to calculate backup navigations in case the digital computers failed, and she was so good at this job that astronaut John Glenn refused to fly on his historic complete orbit around the earth unless Katherine was the one to verify the backup calculations.

Over the years, Katherine published many papers and encouraged young people to enter scientific fields. She became an iconic figure when *Hidden Figures*, a film based on Katherine and two other female Black mathematicians, was released in 2016. After her death in February, 2020, she was inducted into the National Women's Hall of Fame. She had launched rockets, yes, but by persevering, she had launched Black women even higher.

As a Black woman working mostly with white men, Katherine felt she had a lot to prove. How do you think she believed in herself?

What might you tell yourself the next time you feel like giving up?

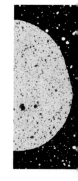

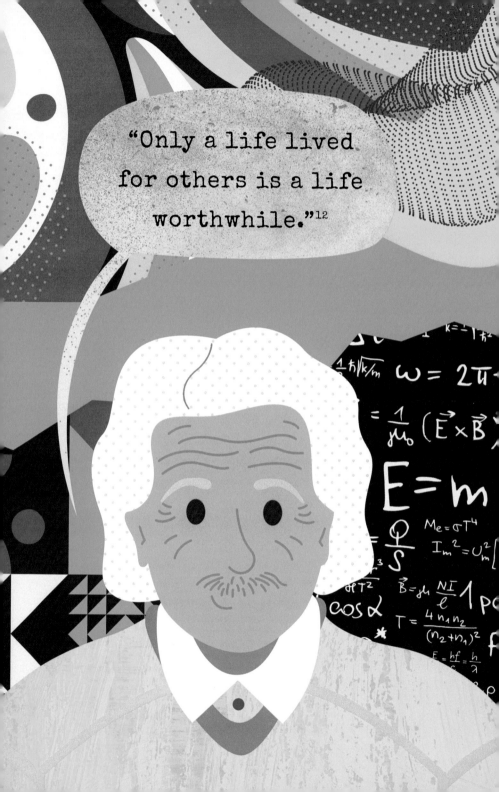

ALBERT EINSTEIN

MARCH 14, 1879-APRIL 18, 1955

The genius who failed his classes.

E ven as a child, Albert Einstein was exception-
ally gifted in math and science. At the age of
twelve, he taught himself algebra and Euclidean
geometry over the space of a single summer. By the
age of fourteen, Albert had mastered both integral
and differential calculus. But although he was
gifted, Albert struggled to get along with most of his
teachers, who he felt stifled his creativity. He scored
well in math and science in advanced testing, but he
failed nearly every other subject.

Despite his difficulties in school, by 1900, at the age of twenty-one, Albert graduated from the Federal Polytechnic School in Zurich, Switzerland. He tried to find work for two years, and he eventually was employed at the Swiss patent office in Bern. It might have seemed like this would be a setback for such a brilliant mind, but it proved to be an important stepping-stone. While working in the patent office, Albert was required to study and answer questions about many topics. There were two in particular that returned frequently to his mind: the transmission of electrical signals, and the electrical-mechanical synchronization of time. As he pondered these topics, he formed thought experiments in his mind that became the basis for some of his greatest future discoveries.

In 1905, Albert received his doctorate from the University of Zurich. Later that year, he published not one but *four* groundbreaking papers. Albert was only twenty-six years old, but these papers and discoveries brought his name to the forefront of academic discussion throughout the entire world.

Over the next thirty years, Albert continued to make advanced scientific progress and traveled the world to work with other scientists. But even Albert wasn't free from opposition. As a Jew, Albert faced discrimination typical of the experiences of other Jews in Europe at the time. By 1933, Nazism had grown and Jews were being persecuted by Hitler's government. Many were killed. Albert decided that it wasn't safe to stay in Europe, so he settled in New Jersey, far away from the home he loved.

Albert's legacy was not just what he did in *spite* of his difficulties, but also what he did *because* of them. The persecution he experienced made him sympathetic toward others who suffered in similar ways, such as Black Americans and refugees of all kinds. His kindness towards all was matched only by his intellectual brilliance.

Albert had to flee his homeland to escape Nazi persecution, but this made him more compassionate. How have you seen your own trials help you develop empathy for others?

Albert's teachers failed him in many subjects, and his parents were worried when he didn't speak until age three. And yet, Albert turned out to have a brilliant mind. Is it possible to misjudge others and not see their potential? Is it possible to not see your own?

TEMPLE GRANDIN

AUGUST 29, 1947–PRESENT

The scientist with a superpower.

The doctors of the 1950s didn't really understand what autism was, so Mary Temple Grandin was incorrectly diagnosed as "brain-damaged" in her childhood. Temple's mother worked hard to make sure that her daughter had safe spaces and access to education just like other children. Based on the advice of disability experts and teachers of the time, her mother was the first person to diagnose her correctly.

Temple had a happy childhood, but junior high and high school were some of the most unpleasant times of her life. She was bullied by her classmates, and at one point, she was expelled from her junior high school when she threw a book at a girl who had been taunting her. The year after her expulsion, Temple spent the summer in Arizona at her step-aunt's cattle ranch, where she studied the behavior of the animals she saw there. She noticed that like her, the cattle often felt threatened by their surroundings and reacted violently to such anxiety-inducing situations.

Temple attended a boarding school for children with behavioral problems during her high school years. A science teacher and former NASA scientist, William Carlock, became her mentor and helped her build her self-confidence. He supported and encouraged Temple as she invented, built, and used the first "hug box." Inspired by the squeeze chutes used to calm cattle while they were vaccinated against diseases, the hug box helped her to calm down by applying physical pressure similar to a hug but without the anxiety that often accompanied human interaction.

Temple completed high school and college, earning a degree in human psychology, and went on to obtain a master's degree and a doctorate in animal science. She used her experiences with her aunt's cattle ranch to develop humane facilities for cattle in livestock ranches. She also began studying the human mind to understand why her thought process seemed different from others'. Temple's discoveries helped her understand animals and understand herself, and she began to speak publicly about autism. Many people have been inspired by her example and openness on the subject, and she continues to raise awareness for both autism and the humane treatment of animals today.

Temple was called "brain-damaged" as a child, but it turns out that autism was a superpower that aided her discoveries about people and animals. Do you have a secret superpower?

Temple speaks often to help people understand those with autism. She turned her challenge into a way to help other people. How might you be able to do the same?

BETHANY HAMILTON

FEBRUARY 8, 1990–PRESENT

The champion surfer who started over.

Bethany Hamilton started surfing the waves of Hawaii when she was only eight years old. She quickly showed a talent for it. By the time she was nine, she was already sponsored in competitions. Everything seemed to be going right, but that was all about to change.

When Bethany was thirteen years old, she went surfing one late October morning with her best friend and her best friend's father and brother. A fourteen-foot-long tiger shark attacked her and bit off most of her left arm below the shoulder. Her friend's family helped put a tourniquet on her arm and called emergency services. Bethany had lost a lot of blood, but fortunately, once she was in the hospital, the doctors were able to close the wound. She eventually healed, but she had lost her arm forever.

Undaunted, Bethany was determined to keep surfing. Just a month after the shark attack, she was back out on the waves. At first, she found it difficult. Without the weight of her arm, her balance was thrown off and she had to re-learn how to surf. She tried using a custom-made board with a handle for her right hand, but over time, Bethany slowly went back to using standard competitive surfboards.

On January 10, 2004—just a little over two months after the shark attack—Bethany entered

Just a month after the shark attack, she was back out on the waves.

her first competition with only one arm. She didn't win that day, but she did well in the competition and knew that she would still be able to keep participating in professional surfing.

Bethany has gone on to win many competitions over the years. She has written books about her experiences and spoken to people all around the world. Despite the traumatic loss of a limb at such an early age, Bethany had the grit to start all over again and become the champion she'd dreamed of.

Bethany was well on her way to becoming a famous surfer when the shark attack happened. She could have given up, but she decided to learn surfing all over again with new balance. What do you think gave her the determination to start over?

Life has many surprises. Some seem good, while others seem hard. In the moment of a hardship, it might seem like everything is ruined. You might feel like giving up! What can you learn from Bethany's life to help you through those moments?

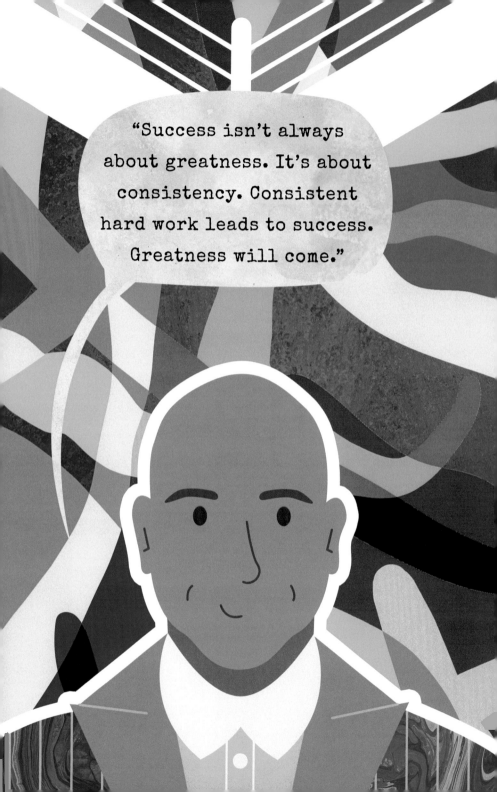

DWAYNE "THE ROCK" JOHNSON

MAY 2, 1972–PRESENT

The wrestler who turned a rough start to stardom.

J ohnson got in trouble as a kid—and that's putting it rather mildly. Before he was seventeen years old, he was arrested several times for fighting, theft, and fraud. But he also played football and rugby and did track and field and wrestling. He was able to earn several athletic scholarships for college and decided to go to the University of Miami.

After Dwayne finished college, he signed a contract with the World Wrestling Federation and became a professional wrestler like his father and grandfather. At first, he was known as "Rocky Maivia," a combination of his father's and grandfather's names, and was promoted as a "face," which meant he played a good character. But after initial successes, fans began to turn on Dwayne. They shouted mean things when he was in the ring and were openly hostile.

After some time, Dwayne turned "heel," or began playing a bad character. He stopped answering to the name "Rocky Maivia" and became known simply as "The Rock." Over the following years in his wrestling career, "The Rock" would switch from being a heel to a face and back again several more times. He grew

Where you start doesn't have to be where you end up.

more famous and popular, even as a heel—audiences began to cheer for him instead of booing him.

In the early 2000s, Dwayne decided to become an actor. Some of his movie credits over the years include *Race to Witch Mountain, Moana, Jumanji: Welcome to the Jungle*, and a recurring role as Luke Hobbs in the long-running Fast & Furious series.

Today, Dwayne is a well-known and much-loved celebrity around the world. He uses his celebrity status to do good things, like his foundation to help terminally ill children and his work with the Make-a-Wish Foundation. From a rocky start to stardom, Dwayne showed the world that where you start doesn't have to be where you end up.

Dwayne made several important decisions that changed the course of his life. Can you identify what some of them were? How do you think he found the courage to change direction from what he was doing before?

Have you ever felt like you were stuck in a certain path in life? What do you learn from Dwayne's life that might help in those circumstances?

HELEN KELLER

JUNE 27, 1880-JUNE 1, 1968

The blind woman who helped others to see.

When Helen Keller was just a baby, she got sick, which caused her to become blind and deaf. Her family was devastated, and over the next seven years, they struggled to communicate with her. Eventually, they hired Anne Sullivan, who was also partly blind, to come and teach Helen. Helen was frustrated at first with her inability to communicate, but it only took a month before Anne was able to teach Helen her first word: water.

Helen and Anne left Helen's home in 1888 so that she could begin attending a special school, the Perkins Institute for the Blind. Helen would also later attend the Wright-Humason School for the Deaf, the Horace Mann School for the Deaf, The Cambridge School for Young Ladies, and Radcliffe College of Harvard University. Helen was the first deaf-blind person to earn a bachelor of arts degree.

Though she could not see or hear and had no experience with how other people saw or heard, Helen was determined to learn to speak. As she later wrote, "One can never consent to creep when one feels an impulse to soar."[16] Over the years, she learned how to communicate by finger-spelling, by reading Braille, and by touching the throat and lips of people who were speaking to her so that she could feel the vibrations and movements and understand what they were saying.

Helen would go on to become a motivational speaker, teacher, and author. For the rest of her life, she would speak up in defense of the blind, the deaf, the disabled, women, people of color, and the poor. She is remembered as a person who taught the world to look at things from a new perspective. "Although the world is full of suffering," she wrote, "it is full also of the overcoming of it. My optimism, then, does not rest on the absence of evil, but on a glad belief in the preponderance of good and a willing effort always to cooperate with the good, that it may prevail."[17]

Helen felt deep compassion for people who might have seemed different to others. How do you think her experiences as a deaf-blind person helped her develop that?

Helen inspired people to overcome their challenges. She also taught them to not take their gifts and senses for granted. What unique lessons might you be able to teach others because of *your* experiences?

Helen was remarkably hopeful and optimistic. Do you think that was despite her challenges or because of them? How can difficult experiences make a person more positive?

LI WENLIANG

OCTOBER 12, 1985–FEBRUARY 7, 2020

The doctor who gave his all to fight COVID-19.

L i Wenliang received his medical degree in 2011 and soon began working as a doctor at Wuhan Central Hospital in Wuhan, China.

In late 2019, doctors in Wuhan began to notice many cases of what they believed was pneumonia. The Wuhan Center for Disease Control sent a memo to all of the hospitals in the province to alert them to the high number of cases. Meanwhile, it also began to investigate the cause of the illness.

Wenliang saw a patient's report that showed that the patient had tested positive for a SARS (severe acute respiratory syndrome) coronavirus. He was concerned and sent a message in a group text to some of his classmates from medical school to let them know that several SARS cases were reported at his hospital. He suggested to his friends that they should let their friends and families know and should take protective measures. Wenliang also asked them to keep this information to themselves, as he wasn't supposed to share it.

However, screenshots of his messages were shared on the Chinese Internet and gained a lot of attention. The supervision department of his hospital blamed him for leaking the information, and he received a warning from the police: if he shared further information about the rapidly increasing cases of coronavirus, he would be prosecuted. However, Wenliang was concerned about the information that was being withheld from the public. On January 31, 2020, he published his experience and the letter of admonition on social media. His post went viral, and the public wondered why his warnings had been censored by the authorities.

Wenliang was worried that the hospital would punish him for "spreading rumors," but his worries were relieved when the Chinese Supreme People's Court stated that he and other citizens who had tried to warn others about the coronavirus should not have been punished for telling the truth.

Unfortunately, Wenliang's work and proximity to the coronavirus cases caused him to contract the illness. He did his best to fight the infection, but he ultimately died of what is now known to be COVID-19 on February 7, 2020. The citizens of Wuhan, the originating city of the virus, were grateful for his attempts to protect them. They placed flowers and blew whistles at Wuhan Central Hospital as a tribute to him. Many people left messages on his social media account, mourning his death.

Despite the threat of punishment in censorship-heavy China, Wenliang was brave enough to speak out about both COVID-19 and about the threats he had received for sharing this information. Wuhan—and the world—are forever grateful.

It was very risky to share information about COVID-19 when the Chinese government didn't want it spread. What do you think gave Wenliang the grit to do so anyway?

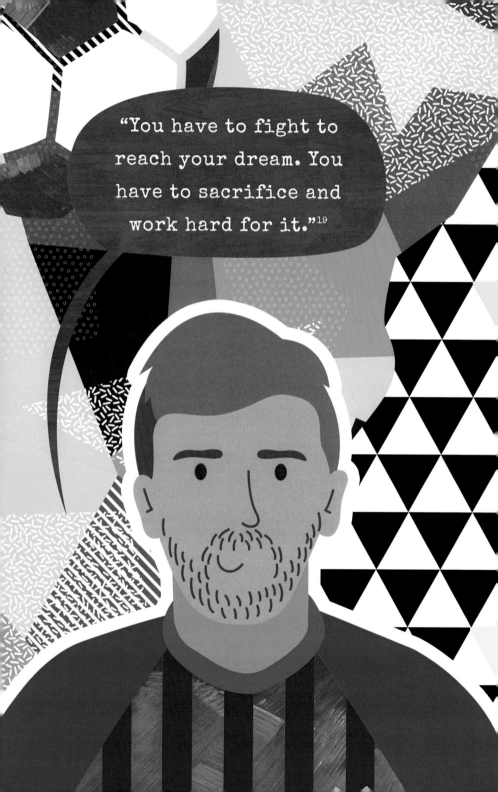

LIONEL MESSI

JUNE 24, 1987–PRESENT

The footballer who found strength in weakness.

I n Rosario, Argentina, Lionel Messi grew up with a strong love for football (called soccer in the United States). He played with his older brothers and cousins and even joined the Newell's Old Boys club when he was just six years old.

Lionel dreamed of becoming a professional football player, but when he was ten years old, he was diagnosed with a growth hormone deficiency, which can cause someone to grow slower and smaller than other people—potentially catastrophic for a would-be footballer. Lionel's father's health insurance would cover only two years of growth hormone treatment, which was very expensive. Newell's agreed to cover the rest of the treatment, but later went back on their word. Lionel was scouted by another football club, River Plate, but they were also unable to pay for Lionel's growth hormone treatment.

In order to give Lionel better opportunities, his family arranged for him to try out with Futbol Club Barcelona in Spain. Most of the directors were hesitant, but eventually they decided to sign Lionel, and he and his family moved to the city of Barcelona. At first, there were some difficulties with Lionel's contract, and he wasn't able to play in many matches and thus struggled to make friends. He was very quiet, to the point that some of his teammates even believed he was mute. His mother and siblings eventually moved back to Argentina and Lionel grew homesick.

Eventually, the contract was fixed and Lionel was able to play. When he was fourteen years old, he finally finished the growth hormone treatments and became part of the "Baby Dream Team," or

Barcelona's elite junior team. During his first full season he was the top scorer, with thirty-six goals.

Still, despite the growth hormone treatment, Lionel's initial deficiency left him quite short and thin. He only grew to become five feet and seven inches tall, but he worked hard to develop muscle and endurance to compensate. He quickly rose through the ranks of the junior teams and even began to play a few games with the main teams just before his eighteenth birthday, when he signed his first adult contract with Barcelona.

Today, Lionel is considered one of the greatest football players in the world and holds many scoring records. He turned a hormone deficiency that might have seemed like the end of his sports career into drive to be the best in the world. That's grit!

What if Lionel hadn't been born with a growth hormone deficiency? Is it possible that the challenge made him work harder than he would have if things were easier?

Think of a challenge that you might have. Can you see ways that your challenge might actually help you?

FLORENCE NIGHTINGALE

MAY 12, 1820–AUGUST 13, 1910

The nurse who blazed her own trail.

lorence Nightingale and her older sister, Frances Parthenope, received high-quality education at a time when many girls and women did not have access to it. They studied history, math, literature, and philosophy, and they learned to speak Italian. Florence in particular showed a talent for research and scientific studies.

Florence decided that she wanted to become a nurse and announced her decision to her family in 1844. Her mother and sister were angry, but she went ahead with it anyway. She had several suitors who wished to marry her, but she knew that because of the social expectations for married women at the time she lived, a marriage would interfere with her nursing ambitions. Fortunately, Florence's family was well-off, and her father supported her ambitions, even providing her with a monthly income so that she could live comfortably while she pursued her career.

In 1854, Florence, along with the rest of Great Britain, learned of the horrific conditions for the wounded at the military hospitals during the Crimean War. She assembled a team of volunteer nurses and traveled to Constantinople (now Istanbul, Turkey) to help. Upon arriving, Florence discovered that the medical staff at the military hospitals were overworked and that there wasn't enough medicine or supplies to keep medical practices hygienic. Illnesses like typhus, typhoid, cholera, and dysentery were more common than battle wounds. Death rates were high; at one point, it was estimated that nearly half of all soldiers who were hospitalized would end up dying. The higher ranking officers seemed indifferent to the suffering of patients and staff alike, so Florence took matters into her own hands. She wrote to the British newspaper *The Times* and made a public plea for government assistance. In response, the British government sent supplies and equipment to set up a new field hospital.

Florence set many new rules about medical care that remain in place today. She was one of the first nurses to implement handwashing and other hygienic practices like cleaner air, better hospital design, and improved conditions for staff. Her efforts resulted in a drastic decrease in death rates.

The British Empire recognized Florence's discoveries and hard work and helped her set up the Nightingale Training School, a nursing school, in 1860. Students at the Nightingale Training School would go on to form nursing schools in other countries. She couldn't have known it at the time, but Florence's dogged determination to follow a path of her own has since saved the lives of millions.

Florence's life followed a path that was very unconventional for the time. Have you ever wanted to try a new path? What might be holding you back? What might be your inspiration to try anyway?

MALALA YOUSAFZAI

JULY 12, 1997-PRESENT

The student who wouldn't be intimidated.

Malala Yousafzai was born in Mingora, Pakistan. Her family ran schools in the area and they believed that education was important for everybody. In early 2009, when she was just eleven years old, she wrote a blog for BBC Urdu under a false name. In the blog, she spoke about her life under the harsh rule of the Taliban and what it was like to speak up about the importance of education for both boys and girls. The blog grew quite famous, and Malala began to give interviews for newspapers and television.

The Taliban did not like what Malala was saying, and she began to receive death threats. In 2012, when Malala was just fifteen, the Taliban sent an assassin to kill her as she was riding the bus home after taking a test. The assassin demanded to know which of the girls on the bus was Malala and threatened to kill all of them. Once he learned who Malala was, the assassin shot her in the head and wounded two other girls. Malala was rushed to the hospital. For some time, the hospital was worried not only that she might die, but that the Taliban might send another assassin. Fortunately, Malala recovered well. She had to have multiple surgeries in order to rebuild her skull and restore her hearing with a cochlear implant.

When Malala's injuries made international news, many people were outraged on her behalf. People in Pakistan held protests against the shooting, and the government offered a reward for information about the attackers. Many political figures, such as United Nations Secretary Ban Ki-moon and former US President Barack Obama, spoke up in support of Malala. The UN Special Envoy for Global Education and former British Prime Minister Gordon Brown even visited Malala in the hospital.

Malala continued her education in Great Britain, where she had been moved for medical treatment after the shooting. She studied hard and did well in school, graduating from high school in 2017 and university in 2020. She also met with Queen Elizabeth II and President Barack Obama and spoke before the United Nations, where she told the assembled leaders that "one child, one teacher, one book, and one pen can change the world."[22] In 2014, Malala was announced as the co-recipient of the Nobel Peace Prize. Her hard work and courageous example have helped children around the world gain access to education and better the lives of themselves and their families.

Malala was nearly killed for supporting education, but that didn't stop her. What do you think gave her the courage to keep speaking out?

By trying to silence Malala, the Taliban ended up making her more influential than ever. Can you think of times that things didn't go right in your life? Is it possible that some obstacles can actually turn into springboards?

ROBERT SCHUMANN

JUNE 8, 1810-JULY 29, 1856

The pianist who created beauty from sorrow.

obert Schumann was born in Zwickau, Germany. As a child, he loved music and literature. With the encouragement of his father, he began to study music when he was just seven years old. Robert was a prodigy, composing songs and pieces that often disregarded musical theory and rules of composition but that were nevertheless advanced for a child of his age. He even wrote and published an essay about the aesthetic of music at the age of fourteen. Robert read often, and in high school, he studied poet-philosophers like Johann Schiller and Johann Goethe.

Robert's father died when Robert was just sixteen. His family pressured him to pursue a career other than music, and in 1828, he traveled to the University of Leipzig to study law. However, Robert couldn't give up piano and he ended up studying music, too. He met his future wife, Clara Wieck, when she performed one of his pieces at a recital, and he would go on to become a beloved composer.

Robert's famous compositions express an unusually wide range of mood and tone, and some of his genius in music might have been an unexpected gift from health challenges he experienced throughout his life. Most of the time he was an adult, Robert suffered through episodes that modern psychologists now believe may have been schizophrenia or bipolar disorder. Other reports suggest he may have had a sort of tumor in his brain that caused hallucinations. Whatever the cause, the episodes were deeply distressing to Robert, and it was a challenge that never left him. Robert poured his sorrow into creating beautiful music with unparalleled depth and emotion. As he once wrote, "Sometimes I am so full of music and so overflowing with melody that I find it simply impossible to write down anything."[24]

Today, people all over the world still love to hear *Papillons, Carnaval,* and Robert's *Piano Concerto in A minor.* His enchanting music is at once hopeful and sorrowful, happy and poignant—a friend by one's side to remind them that one person, at least, knows what it is to feel deep emotion. And in a world that desperately needs empathy, there might be no greater gift.

Robert turned his sadness into something beautiful. Have you ever experienced something sorrowful? Are there ways your experience helped other parts of your life feel more rich and beautiful?

Many things in life are like a coin: for every difficult side, there is something on the other side that brings something good. Think about some of the difficult things you have experienced. What are some of the good things that might have come along with them?

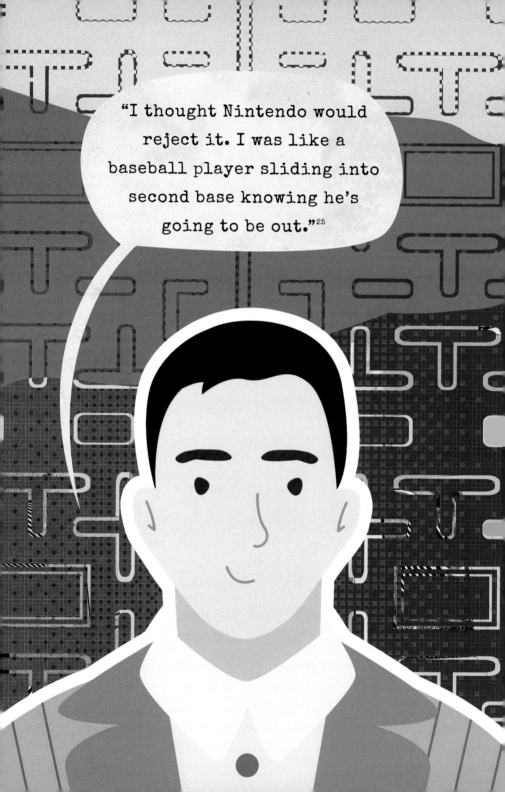

SAT●SHI
TAJIRI

AUGUST 28, 1965-PRESENT

The game creator who never quit.

S atoshi Tajiri grew up in Machida, a suburb of Tokyo, Japan. He spent much of his childhood outside in nature and enjoyed insect collecting as a hobby. Other children even nicknamed him "Mr. Bug." As a teenager, Satoshi developed an interest in video games and arcade games. He took apart his own Nintendo Entertainment System just to see how it worked. Sometimes Satoshi would skip school to play video games, but he eventually made up all of his work and graduated from high school.

From 1981 to 1986, Satoshi wrote, edited, and published a fan magazine focused on arcade video games. The fanzine was named *Game Freak* and was handwritten and stapled together. An illustrator named Ken Sugimori joined him to produce the art. Over time, after writing stories about so many different games, the two of them realized that most video games were not very good quality. They decided to try to develop their own video games and took the name "Game Freak" with them as the name of their new company.

When Satoshi learned about Nintendo's Game Boy console and its Link Cable system whereby two players could connect their consoles and play a game together, he imagined little bugs crawling back and forth between the wires. It reminded him of his childhood and love of collecting insects. He realized that the Link Cable system would work well for video game players to trade collectible game items with one another. Soon, in 1990, the idea for Pocket Monsters, or Pokémon for short, was born.

Satoshi pitched the idea to Nintendo. They were intrigued but felt the concept needed more work. Satoshi, Ken, and the other employees of Game

Freak spent the next six years working on the first Pokémon games. The company nearly went bankrupt several times, and Satoshi himself did not take a salary. Several employees quit, and they even had to borrow money from another game development company. However, they finally finished the games, and *Pokémon Red* and *Pokémon Green* (known as *Pokémon Blue* in other countries) were published in 1996. Most people, including Satoshi himself, were not expecting the Pokémon games to do very well. But over time, the games grew to be very popular; in fact, they quickly became one of the top-selling games in Nintendo's lineup.

Today, Pokémon is massively popular, both in Japan and in nearly every other country around the world. It has inspired video games, movies, trading cards, toys, and plushies. Through hard work and sacrifice, Satoshi Tajiri's childhood dream became one of the top-selling media franchises of all time.

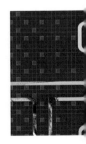

Satoshi faced many obstacles while trying to launch Pokémon. Why don't you think he gave up? What do you think kept him going, even without pay?

About the Author

S.E. ABRAMSON graduated from Brigham Young University in 2016 with a BA in English. She lives in south-central Pennsylvania with her family. She enjoys writing, video games, and anthroponomastics.

If you liked this book, please leave a review online at your favorite retailer. Honest reviews spread the word about Bushel & Peck—and help us make better books, too!

About Bushel & Peck Books

BUSHEL & PECK BOOKS is a children's publishing house with a special mission. Through our Book-for-Book Promise™, we donate one book to kids in need for every book we sell. Our beautiful books are given to kids through schools, libraries, local neighborhoods, shelters, nonprofits, and also to many selfless organizations that are working hard to make a difference. So thank you for purchasing this book! Because of you, another book will make its way into the hands of a child who needs it most.

Nominate a school or organization to receive free books

Do you know a school, library, or organization that could use some free books for their kids? We'd love to help! Please fill out the nomination form on our website, and we'll do everything we can to make something happen.

www.bushelandpeckbooks.com/pages/
nominate-a-school-or-organization

Notes

1. "Grit." 2021. *Merriam-Webster*. https://www.merriam-webster.com/dictionary/grit.
2. Beethoven's epigraph to "String Quartet No. 16 in F major, Op. 135." (In German, it originally read: *Muss es sein? Es muss sein!*)
3. Rolland, Romain. *Portrait of Beethoven in His Thirtieth Year*. 1929.
4. Owens, Jesse. 1970. *Blackthink*. William Morrow.
5. Boom, Corrie ten, John L. Sherrill, and Elizabeth Sherrill. 1974. *The Hiding Place: The Triumphant True Story of Corrie ten Boom*. New York: Bantam.
6. Blackwell Family. *Blackwell Family Papers: Elizabeth Blackwell Papers, -1946*; Speech, Article, and Book File, 1857 to 1916; Address on the Medical Education of Women New York: Baptist & Taylor, 1864, 16 pp. 1864. Manuscript/Mixed Material. https://www.loc.gov/item/mss1288001236/.
7. Ibid.
8. "Ellen Degeneres." 2009. S24E41. *The Oprah Winfrey Show*.
9. Carter, Bill. 1994. "At Lunch With: Ellen DeGeneres; Dialed God (Pause). He Laughed." *The New York Times*. April 13.
10. "Our American Culture." 1941. *The Metropolitan Opera*.
11. Wild, Flint. 2015. "Katherine Johnson: A Lifetime of STEM." NASA. November 16. https://www.nasa.gov/audience/foreducators/a-lifetime-of-stem.html.
12. Bassuk, Albert. 1932. "Einstein Is Terse in Rule for Success;" *The New York Times*. June 20. https://www.nytimes.com/1932/06/20/archives/einstein-is-terse-in-rule-for-success-only-life-lived-for-others-is.html.
13. Silberman, Steve. 2015. *NeuroTribes*. Penguin Publishing Group.
14. Hamilton, Bethany, Shery Berk, and Rick. Bundschuh. 2006. *Soul Surfer: a True Story of Faith, Family, and Fighting to Get Back on the Board*. New York: MTV Books.
15. Keller, Helen. *Optimism*. 1903.
16. Keller, Helen. *The Story of My Life*. 1903.
17. Keller, Helen. *Optimism*. 1903.
18. Jianhang, Qin, and Timmy Shen. 2020. "Rebuked Coronavirus Whistleblower Vindicated by Top Chinese Court." *Nikkei Asia*. February 5. https://asia.nikkei.com/Spotlight/Caixin/Rebuked-coronavirus-whistleblower-vindicated-by-top-Chinese-court.
19. Agence France-Presse. 2013. "Football: Messi Says 'Sacrifice' Took Him to the Top." Inquirer.net. August 7. https://sports.inquirer.net/113053/football-messi-says-sacrifice-took-him-to-the-top.
20. Nightingale, Florence. *Cassandra*. 1860.
21. Schaub, Michael. 2015. "Malala Yousafzai Wants Leaders to Invest in #Booksnotbullets." *Los Angeles Times*. July 8. https://www.latimes.com/books/jacketcopy/la-et-jc-malala-yousafzai-books-not-bullets-20150708-story.html.
22. "Malala Yousafzai: 16th Birthday Speech at the United Nations: Malala Fund Newsroom." 2021. Malala Fund | Newsroom. https://malala.org/newsroom/archive/malala-un-speech.
23. Dwight, John Sullivan. 1856. *Dwight's Journal of Music*.
24. Schumann, Clara. *Early Letters of Robert Schumann*. 1888.
25. Chua-Eoan, Howard and Tim Larimer. 1999. "Beware of the Poke Mania." *Time*. November 22. http://content.time.com/time/subscriber/article/0,33009,992625-5,00.html.

Printed in the United States
by Baker & Taylor Publisher Services